A FAN'S GUIDE TO UNDERSTANDING THE NFL SALARY CAP

HOW THE NFL SALARY CAP WORKS AND WHY IT MATTERS

BRUCE IRONS

WOLF MOUNTAIN
- PUBLISHING -

ISBN 978-1-952286-10-0 (paperback)

ISBN 978-1-952286-11-7 (ebook)

"It doesn't take a 'cap guru' or 'cap wizard' to constantly restructure and push out cap charges to bring down the current cap.

It takes a cap guru or cap wizard to not have to do that."

- Andrew Brandt, former Director of Player Finance for the Green Bay Packers

CONTENTS

DEDICATION

Dedicated to the men who risk their lives and physical well-being so we can be entertained on Sundays, and to Andy, Mike, and Dustin for talking to me about it too much.

INTRODUCTION

Do you like football? Do you like watching your team every Sunday in the fall? Do you want a deeper understanding of how your team was built? Do you want to appreciate the game a little more?

Then this is the book for you!

You know how most articles that try to explain the NFL Collective Bargaining Agreement (CBA) are just vague statements cut and paste from other articles that only touch on a piece of the big picture and leave you with more questions than answers?

Me too!

I hate that, so here is the definitive guide to understanding the NFL salary cap.

We'll cover everything about how the NFL salary cap works and how it shapes NFL teams. We'll see real examples of how teams structure contracts and why, and we'll get deep into the ways teams manage contract structures under their cap to field the best team possible.

If you ever wondered why your team didn't sign a player who would have been a perfect fit or why they cut a guy in the middle of his contract even though he was playing fine, this book will help you understand.

This is the game behind the game.

These questions have answers that go beyond the x's and o's of strategy, and they're the answers that provide the deepest understanding of this intoxicating sport.

The answers lie in the mechanics of the salary cap.

The salary cap is why your team didn't sign that free agent that could have put them over the top. The salary cap is why that veteran player, who did just fine, and leaves dead money on your team's cap, still had to be cut.

Unfortunately, the salary cap - the most important piece to building an NFL team - is the most misunderstood aspect of the game by fans.

If you truly want to understand this game, this is the book for you.

PART I

HOW THE CBA AND THE SALARY CAP WORK

1

WELCOME

W elcome to A Fan's Guide To Understanding The NFL Salary Cap.

Get ready to understand the NFL salary cap at a level no other resource takes fans through.

We really hope you enjoy it. Now, the key to any best-selling book is to grip a reader in the early pages.

Sorry, we can't do that here.

This isn't a Dean Koontz thriller or even a Danielle Steele chick lit, this is the business side of football - where the game begins.

For some, this might not be exciting.

It is, however, fascinating.

If you're like me, you picked up this book because you love football and want to understand it better. You see conflicting reports on social media and you read a bunch of vague articles about the CBA that leave you with more questions than answers. Then you see all these crazy headlines on sensationalist websites that don't make sense.

This is the book to help you understand clearly and factually how these things work.

If you want to understand the salary cap so you can understand how football really works, you have to understand how the CBA works. I'll try to make it sound exciting, but this is the fine print portion of understanding how the cap works (and, more importantly, *why* it works the way it does).

You can skip ahead to get to chapters that look more interesting if you want, but you'll probably miss some of the fundamentals. You can stop reading and return this book right now if that doesn't interest you.

But I think you'll be missing out.

I think you're here because your curiosity is piqued about a critical part of the modern NFL. That thing you hear so much about and kinda get, but don't fully understand. That thing that isn't really clearly explained anywhere.

You're here because you want to fully understand it so you can fully appreciate how great and complex the back side of football is. You're here to understand and appreciate the game.

If not, that's cool, too.

But if you're still here, open your mind and get ready!

You've been warned.

2

UNDERSTANDING THE CBA

The Collective Bargaining Agreement (CBA) is the contract between the NFL Owners and The NFL Players that defines how they will do business together (not every one of them signs - there's a bunch of lawyers and fine print, but that's the gist of it).

The NFL is made up of 32 teams. They're 32 individual operating companies that agree to do business the same way under the umbrella of the NFL.

Now, if McDonald's, Burger King, Wendy's, and Hardee's all got together and said they were going to pay their employees the same way and not let them choose which business they wanted to work for, that would be illegal.

In the United States, people get to choose which company they want to work for. When companies behave like I described above, it's a violation of antitrust laws (the laws that make sure we have a free market economy with open competition that benefits consumers like you and me).

In most major sports, including football, leagues operate with an antitrust exemption. This means some of the rules and protections for normal, non-millionaire-superstar-athletes don't apply to these millionaire-super-star-athletes.

This antitrust exemption means that, even though there are 32 NFL teams all operating as independent companies, the players (a type of employee) don't get as much of a say in their employment as someone working at McDonald's.

If you work at McDonald's and you don't like it, you can just quit and go work at Burger King. Things aren't quite the same in the NFL. Players work under contracts that specify which team they will play for and for how long (players can throw a fit and hold out for a better contract or refuse to report to camp, but those are exceptions outside of the defined rules, so we won't cover those here).

NFL players are unionized, however, and as a collective group, that union, known as the NFL Players Association (NFLPA), negotiates with the owners of the NFL teams to define the CBA, which is the generally agreed upon rules that owners and players will abide by and negotiate under for the purpose of doing business.

The CBA defines things like safety regulations, retirement benefits, and healthcare reimbursement accounts.

We're going to skip all that boring stuff in this book to focus on one piece of the CBA: the salary cap.

3

THE SALARY CAP

Think of the salary cap like an allowance, but instead of getting $20 a week for loading the dishwasher and picking up dog poop, you get $200,000,000 to field a competitive football team.

The cap defines the upper limit of what a team can spend on its players. This is to prevent a big market team with a very rich or aggressive owner from simply buying a championship by out-spending all the other teams to get the best players.

That wouldn't be fun.

The salary cap exists for two primary reasons: to establish parity and limit owner risk.

Limiting owner risk is a very straightforward proposition (even if it gets less press than creating parity - which owners would have you believe is the primary or sole goal of the salary cap). Not only does the salary cap limit (or "cap") the amount owners can spend, the cap itself is determined by league revenue. The CBA states that the salary cap is determined by splitting about 48% of the league's total revenue by 32.

That means if, oh let's say a global pandemic, for example, hits, and league revenue drops, the salary cap drops as well. This means that the owners can't lose money.

It's a brilliant play on the part of the billionaires' lawyers.

The cap also establishes parity, which is what we, as fans, should care about.

Establishing parity is a big part of what makes football the most compelling, entertaining, and successful sport in America. Nobody wants to see a league dominated by a dynasty while their team languishes in mediocrity because they can't outspend the bigger markets. The cap fixes that.

The NFL has far stricter salary cap rules than the NBA or MLB. NFL teams can shift money around and massage the cap hits (which we'll get into in depth in Part 2), but in the NFL, you have to count every dollar paid to a player against the cap at some point.

Major League Baseball doesn't have a salary cap. This makes for all sorts of crazy scenarios. Heading into the 2020 MLB season, the New York Yankees had a payroll of over $240M - almost a quarter of a billion dollars - while the Miami Marlins had a payroll under $45M. MLB's luxury tax model means that a team can try to outspend all the other teams to put together an unstoppable squad and try to buy a title.

The NBA kind of has a "salary cap", but also has a luxury tax model like MLB, and a bunch of other exceptions allow owners to spend more and shift the competitive balance. And since there's only five players from each team on the court at a time, it's a lot easier to build a super-team. Free agents figured this out in 2010, when back-to-back MVP LeBron James and four-time All-Star Chris Bosh both decided to join six-time All-Star Dwyane Wade on the Miami Heat.

This makes the game less enjoyable for fans when there is a clear delineation between haves and have-nots... especially when your team is a have-not.

Every dollar that is paid to players in the NFL has to count against the cap at some point. This means base salaries, this means signing bonuses, this means performance incentives, this means practice squad players - every dollar that is paid out counts against the cap and makes sure that teams can't outspend each other.

When teams have a limit on what they can spend, no one can buy a title.

But what if teams go the opposite way? What if a team didn't want to spend anything? A hapless team of minimum-contract undrafted free agents would be no fun, either.

That brings us to our next point...

Minimum Spending

The cap sets the ceiling on spending, but players wouldn't be very happy if teams all stopped offering big contracts, especially if perennial losers just wanted to eke out a profit or rebuilding teams went into tank mode.

This would swing parity and competitive balance in

the wrong direction as weak teams wouldn't be able to put up a fight. Worse yet for the players: they wouldn't be getting paid as much!

To make sure that doesn't happen, players (and their lawyers) insisted on league minimum spending requirements in the CBA.

Every CBA is signed for a 10-year term, then a new CBA is signed for another 10-year term. Within each 10-year CBA, there are 3- and 4-year windows. For each 3- or 4-year window within the CBA, each team is required to spend at least 90% of the cumulative salary cap.

This means that if the salary cap was $200M for the first year of the window, $220M for the second year, and $250M for the third year, that each team would be required to spend at least $603M (90% of the total $670M for the 3-year period) over the course of those 3 years. If they spent less than that, the difference would need to be paid out directly to all the players that were on the roster at any point during that period in a prorated allocation.

In addition to that, there is also a requirement that the entire league spends at least 95% of total cap during those windows. That means that if the salary cap was $200M, $220M, and $250M for a three year stretch like above (making the total cap a cool $19.295B - which is $670M times 32 teams), that all the teams combined spending on player contracts would need to be at least $18.3312B (95% of the $19.295B). If they spend less than that, the difference would need to be paid out to all players that were on any roster during that time frame in a prorated allocation.

Sure, the players want to make sure they get as much money as they can. They don't let the teams short change them, but this is also closely related to parity. Making teams all spend within about 5% of each other means there should be some semblance of evenness in the relative competitiveness of each team. This makes the sport more interesting for fans.

Remember at the beginning of the chapter when we talked about the salary cap as being like an allowance?

Well, if you're young enough to have an allowance, odds are good that you won't qualify for a credit card. That means that you can't buy expensive things that cost more than you have. In NFL salary cap terms, this means teams can't borrow money from future years for their salary cap.

You can, however, save money from your allowance to use in future. This is what happens when a team uses less than 100% of their salary cap. They are only required to spend 90% of their cap for a 3-year period, but anything not spent between 90% and 100% doesn't just disappear, it gets saved for next year.

The salary cap is a hard cap, but it's also a bit of a fluid accounting construct that allows for money to be rolled over each year, kinda like if you save your allowance.

Let's say the salary cap is $200M. That means each team gets $200M to spend on players for that season (other expenses - like coaches, executives, and new porta-potties for the tailgate zone - do not count towards the cap).

If a team only spends $180M one year (which, as 90% of $200M is the minimum amount they must spend), they can roll over $20M of cap credit and add it to their "adjusted" cap for the following season. This means that the team would be able to spend $220M the following year if the salary cap were to remain the same at $200M.

The salary cap is based on the total league revenue, though, so the cap can go up each year - and usually does (unless something like an unforeseen pandemic drives revenue down).

Building on the scenario above, if the cap were to increase to $210M the following year, the team that saved $20M the previous year would then have $230M to spend as their adjusted cap.

Then the team would then be required to spend 90% of their unadjusted cap (the base cap number, not including any amount rolled over), or $189M (90% of $210M), for that season.

If the team again spent only the minimum amount, they would rollover $41M (their $230M adjusted cap minus their $189M of spend) to the following year. This can be a big advantage if all the other teams are spending their full cap. The teams with the most money have the best chance of landing free agents.

This is how a team can set themselves up for a big splash in free agency. If one team has saved more money than the others, they will have an advantage in trying to sign free agents.

At the same time, it's hard to field a competitive team if you aren't spending your cap allotment on good players every year.

This is how the fortunes of teams can turn.

It's hard to win in the NFL without at least a good quarterback, so teams without a good quarterback can underspend for a couple of years to build up cap room.

Since they don't have a good quarterback and they aren't spending in free agency, they will probably lose a lot of games and get a high draft pick (you can read more about this in one of my other books: *A Fan's Guide To Understanding The NFL Draft*).

They can use that draft pick on an exciting young quarterback prospect, then spend all that saved up cap space to sign free agents.

It doesn't always work, but it's a logical and often-employed strategy to turn around a franchise.

Teams can save up cap space to try something like this, but they cannot do the opposite. They are not allowed to spend more than the cap one year and then take a cap penalty the following year (i.e., they aren't allowed to use a credit card if their allowance isn't big enough for everything they want to buy).

These are the basic tools that are used to build an NFL team. All the rules are laid out in a CBA that strives to ensure parity or, at the very least, a level playing field.

The owners and players both benefit from this arrangement, but make no mistake about it: the owners are negotiating from a position of strength.

4

WHY THE OWNERS ALWAYS WIN CBA NEGOTIATIONS

Even though the owners and players both have to agree to the CBA, it almost always favors the owners. No matter how high revenues get, the cap (tied to earnings) ensures that owners don't have to spend so much of their income that they become unprofitable. If revenues drop (which seemed unthinkable before a pandemic rocked the 2020 season), the cap drops, which means the minimum spending requirements drop, limiting the risk of the owners and ensuring they stay profitable.

Players on the other hand, have a ton of risk. We'll get deeper into how contracts work in Part 2, but the big factor is that only signing bonuses (which are paid immediately) are guaranteed - everything else in a contract is only paid when it's due. If anything happens before it's due, the player doesn't get paid.

Break your neck and can't play anymore?

No more money.

Lose a step with old age and get cut?

No more money.

Someone posts a video of you doing something you shouldn't be doing and you get cut?

No more money.

So why don't the players - a unionized group of wealthy people represented and counseled by very expensive lawyers - bargain for a better deal?

Because owners can think long-term while players, on the whole, have to think short-term. The owners know this and take full advantage of it.

Let's look at why.

The NFLPA needs a majority vote of all players to approve a CBA.

"All players" includes mega-millionaires like Patrick Mahomes making almost $50M per year, but it also includes guys you never heard of on the practice squad, who make around $142k (if they make it the whole season). Yes, $142k sounds like a lot of money, but after agent fees, union dues, and the costs of maintaining your body to be able to put up with the rigors of the game, it's not the same as making all that money by collecting ad revenue off your kitten videos on YouTube. The guys at the bottom of the NFL pyramid are clawing to earn their money.

Since the CBA the players vote on will last for 10 years, and professional football players have one of the shortest careers of any profession in the world, it's safe to say that most of the players voting on it won't be around by the time it ends.

This is why the players, as a collective, keep getting screwed.

If they took a hardline stance and fought for the things they should have (a 50-50 revenue split, a great retirement health care plan, and no additional games, for starters), they would probably end up missing some games as owners refuse to sign. As a result, the players would lose some money (since they don't get paid if there are no games happening).

Guys like Patrick Mahomes have more than enough money to miss some game checks. Heck, his grandkids can live a life of luxury just off his signing bonus even if he never played again. It's the masses of guys at the bottom of the pyramid that would suffer.

Let's look at it from their perspective.

Let's say I'm a borderline special teams player on a middling squad making the league minimum.

I'm just hoping I can hang on with the team next year, maybe I can make it a couple years and save a little money before I have to get a job at a used car lot and do auto-graph signings at card shows for $50 a day. But if the team changes coaches, changes coordinators, or drafts someone at my position, or I get hurt, or any other of a number of bad things happen, I'm off the team.

No more paychecks.

Just like that.

I'll be a free agent.

I'll look for a new team, but when other teams have the choice between picking up a low-rung veteran like me, or going with a cheap, homegrown undrafted free agent, they almost always go for the latter (they're cheaper, are more familiar with the system, and are usually believed to have more potential).

My career might be over.

That $142k salary - tiny by NFL standards, but rich in the real world - is gone and I may never make anywhere near that in my life again.

My whole goal is to last three or four years in this game so I can scrape together enough money to supplement my future income doing something like selling used cars, so I can have a better life than a guy who has to live solely on the income from selling used cars.

In short, I need to scrape up whatever wages I can. If owners wanna throw an extra game in to get me more money now, I'm in! I don't have long, so I'll take what I can get. The one thing I can't afford is to miss any part of this season - if we hold out, I'm probably done.

Sure, Patrick Mahomes and all the guys with 8 figure annual incomes are probably saying "Hey, let's hold out for a better deal." But they're outnumbered 15 to 1 by guys like me who make less on a 4-year contract than Mahomes makes with a single game check. Those guys, the bottom of the pyramid, the bigger number of masses, are going to vote for a worse deal so they can get something before it's too late.

Those guys rock the vote.

Owners know this.

Owners are thinking longer term. Their career earnings window is ten or twenty times as long as that of most players.

Owners are also rich, meaning they don't care if they miss a few games. Every owner either made a ludicrous amount of money before they bought their team or they inherited the team from parents who made a ludicrous amount of money.

And when I say a ludicrous amount, I'm talking big. Way bigger than what Patrick Mahomes makes as the highest-paid player ever.

Shahid Khan bought the Jaguars in 2011 for $770M, the same year that his company had revenue of $7.5B. That was twice as much as the salary cap for all 32 teams combined that year.

Think about that.

The newest owner, a self-made billionaire with the newest money of them all, had a company that made more than twice as much as all of the players in the entire league combined.

And he's not the richest owner by a long shot.

Guys like that, guys who own a football team as a little side hustle, can afford to miss football income a lot more than some 23-year-old fringe long-snapper.

But those low-end players, the little guys, have a vote that counts just as much as Patrick Mahomes's vote. And there's a lot more of them.

So owners negotiate accordingly.

They offer some crappy terms and tell the players to vote.

The players could either:

A) Vote for the long-term benefit of all players in the future

B) Vote to get some money now before it's too late, knowing full well that if they don't play this year, they may never play again and all that's waiting for them is a job selling used cars

They go with B, every time.

At the time of the 2020 CBA vote, about 60% of players in the NFL were on a league-minimum contract. That's a voting majority. The owners proposed a CBA that increased the minimum salary by 20%.

The vote passed.

It's hard to fault the players for taking a huge pay increase when their careers are so short. Just like it's hard to fault the owners for negotiating from a position of strength.

It's systemic.

This is what happens every single time.

It happened last time.

It happened this time.

It's what will happen next time.

It's a natural progression of the evolution of the sport.

Maybe the only thing that could possibly disrupt it is a rival league offering better benefits and rising in popularity to such a level that it threatens the NFL.

Given the barriers to entry (established fan bases and lucrative TV deals and sponsorships), it may never happen.

We can talk for hours about if this is fair or not, but for now, let's just accept that this is how things are for the context of understanding how the cap works.

PART II

HOW CONTRACTS WORK

5

CONTRACT BASICS

I n Part 1, we talked about how the salary cap works at a high level.

The numbers that fill up the cap are player contracts and there's a lot to know to truly understand how teams are built.

NFL contracts are made up of two pieces: base salary and bonuses.

The base salary is a very straightforward mechanism. Each year, a player is paid a defined amount for that season. The salary is paid out in weekly installments over the 17 weeks of the NFL season. So if a player makes \$1.7M per year in base salary, they will receive it in the form of a \$100k check each week of the regular season. All of the base salary counts against the cap for the year it is paid out.

Bonuses can be a little trickier, especially signing bonuses. We'll get to other bonuses later, but for this section, we'll focus on signing bonus because they'll help us understand how contracts work the best.

The signing bonus, as the name implies, is paid in full immediately when a player signs a contract. It's a big motivator to get a deal done. Hey, player, you don't have to wait for this big chunk of change to be paid out in weekly increments (assuming you're still on the team), you can get a bunch of cash right now!

Players love big signing bonuses. They're paid right away and they're fully guaranteed. Base salary isn't paid out if a player is cut. This makes the balance between base salaries and signing bonuses the biggest factor in how a contract is structured.

It also makes the signing bonus a curious item in the CBA.

Players want big signing bonuses, but if teams have to squeeze a big payment into the salary cap on the first year of a contract, it would make it really hard to give out big signing bonuses.

So owners and players (and their lawyers) agreed in the CBA that signing bonuses could be amortized over the life of the contract. In this book, we'll use the word amortized or prorated, but they mean the same thing: spread the money out. You get the amortized or prorated amount simply by dividing the signing bonus by the number of years on the contract -that's the amount of the bonus that counts against the cap each year.

The signing bonus is paid in full immediately, but the cap hit is spread out over the contract.

This is the basic foundation of NFL contract structures.

It's grade school level math, but the way it gets used in practice jumps to college level accounting.

Let's look at some examples.

Tommy Fullback is a low-end player that isn't in high demand. He signs a 4 year, $4M dollar contract with no signing bonus.

Tommy's contract is all base salary, but it can be structured in any number of ways. He could make the same amount each year, like this:

- Year 1: $1M
- Year 2: $1M
- Year 3: $1M
- Year 4: $1M

Or maybe the team wants to give Tommy a little incentive to sign, since he isn't getting a signing bonus. In that case, they could front-load the contract and put more of the money in earlier years of the deal like this:

- Year 1: $1.2M
- Year 2: $1.1M
- Year 3: $900k
- Year 4: $800k

That could be nice, but maybe the team decides they actually want some security from Tommy - they want to give him an incentive to play out the whole contract. Then, they could back-load the contract and put more money in the later years of the deal like this:

- Year 1: $700k
- Year 2: $700k
- Year 3: $800k
- Year 4: $1.8M

This type of deal gives the team a little more security because, with no signing bonus to worry about, they could cut Tommy after a year or two if he isn't playing great and they wouldn't lose much of an investment since players don't get paid their base salary if they are cut.

Ok, this is basic stuff, right? Relax, we're just easing into this and we want to start with a firm understanding of the mechanics. Let's ramp up the complexity a bit and throw in signing bonuses.

Let's say Stevie Touchdown is a little more in-demand than Tommy Fullback.

Stevie is gonna get a 4 year, $50M contract. Let's say he gets a $10M signing bonus and a $10M salary each year.

Since his signing bonus gets paid immediately, the actual money he is paid would break down like this:

- Year 1: $20M ($10M base salary + $10M signing bonus)
- Year 2: $10M (base salary)
- Year 3: $10M (base salary)
- Year 4: $10M (base salary)

This isn't how the cap is charged, though. Remember, his signing bonus gets prorated, so it's impact to the cap is spread out over the contract. So this is what Stevie's cap charge looks like:

- Year 1: $12.5M ($10M base salary + $2.5M prorated signing bonus)
- Year 2: $12.5M ($10M base salary + $2.5M prorated signing bonus)
- Year 3: $12.5M ($10M base salary + $2.5M prorated signing bonus)
- Year 4: $12.5M ($10M base salary + $2.5M prorated signing bonus)

Nice and easy, right?

It is, but most contracts aren't so clean. Football contracts, like life, can get messy.

Let's say the team has a little extra cap space saved up from rolling some money over last year, but they know that next year, they have a couple key players coming up in free agency. In order to make good use of their extra cap this year, and free up a little extra space for re-signing some guys next year, maybe the team offers Stevie a contract that shifts half of his Year 2 base salary into Year 1.

This allows them to "pre-pay" in a sense so they have more money available next year.

Then, his actual pay would look like this:

- Year 1: $25M ($15M base salary + $10M signing bonus)
- Year 2: $5M (base salary)
- Year 3: $10M (base salary)
- Year 4: $10M (base salary)

And his cap charges would look like this:

- Year 1: $17.5M ($15M base salary + $2.5M prorated signing bonus)
- Year 2: $7.5M ($5M base salary + $2.5M prorated signing bonus)
- Year 3: $12.5M ($10M base salary + $2.5M prorated signing bonus)
- Year 4: $12.5M ($10M base salary + $2.5M prorated signing bonus)

Logical, right?

Now, the team could leave the base salaries the same and just roll that $5M over into next year (assuming they meet the minimum payment thresholds), but this allows them to have cleaner books.

This doesn't happen very often, though. A more common scenario is that the team has been overspending and doesn't have a lot of money this year or next year. In that case, they may offer Stevie $5M base salaries in the first two years, with $15M base salaries in the last two years. This would help them in the short term (and they can worry about the long term later, assuming they aren't fired before then).

In this scenario, Stevie's actual pay would look like this:

- Year 1: $15M ($5M base salary + $10M signing bonus)
- Year 2: $5M (base salary)
- Year 3: $15M (base salary)
- Year 4: $15M (base salary)

And his cap charges would look like this:

- Year 1: $7.5M ($5M base salary + $2.5M prorated signing bonus)
- Year 2: $7.5M ($5M base salary + $2.5M prorated signing bonus)
- Year 3: $17.5M ($15M base salary + $2.5M prorated signing bonus)
- Year 4: $17.5M ($15M base salary + $2.5M prorated signing bonus)

Now, what if the team really likes Stevie and they see him as a long-term fixture on this team? Could they lock him up on an even longer deal and spread out his signing bonus even further?

In theory, they sure could, but there are a couple things to consider. If Stevie settled for a $10M signing bonus for a 4-year deal, he would probably want something like a $20M signing bonus for an 8-year deal. Actually, considering that salaries tend to go up every year, he would probably be looking more in the neighborhood of a $25M signing bonus.

And, since salaries tend to go up over time, Stevie would probably want higher average salaries, too. Think about it from his perspective: if he played out a 4-year deal worth $50M, what kind of deal would he expect to sign after that? If you look at deals that top players signed 4 years ago and compared it to what top players sign for now, you'll probably see a big jump. Stevie is going to believe salaries will be high in the future and will probably want a higher average salary for a longer deal.

So let's say the team agrees that $25M is a reasonable signing bonus for an 8-year deal and that both sides think $10M in base salary for the first 4 years is fair along with $12M in base salary for the final 4 years.

With that all squared away, the sides can sign a contract, but (as Lt. Columbo liked to say) there is just one more thing.

The CBA allows signing bonuses to be prorated over a contract. That proration has to be evenly spread, by the way (teams can't choose to take bigger cap hits from the signing bonus in some years and smaller ones in other years - they have to be equal each year).

Furthermore, the CBA only allows teams to spread out the signing bonus cap hit over 5 years, regardless of how long the contract is for.

That means this scenario would pay Steve like this:

- Year 1: $35M ($10M base salary + $25M signing bonus)
- Year 2: $10M (base salary)
- Year 3: $10M (base salary)
- Year 4: $10M (base salary)
- Year 5: $12M (base salary)
- Year 6: $12M (base salary)
- Year 7: $12M (base salary)
- Year 8: $12M (base salary)

While his cap charges would look like this:

- Year 1: $15M ($10M base salary + $5M prorated signing bonus)

- Year 2: $15M ($10M base salary + $5M prorated signing bonus)
- Year 3: $15M ($10M base salary + $5M prorated signing bonus)
- Year 4: $15M ($10M base salary + $5M prorated signing bonus)
- Year 5: $17M ($12M base salary + $5M prorated signing bonus)
- Year 6: $12M (base salary)
- Year 7: $12M (base salary)
- Year 8: $12M (base salary)

It doesn't matter if a player signs a deal for 100 years, the signing bonus has to be paid immediately and the cap hit can only be spread out for a maximum of 5 years.

This helps establish parity by keeping teams' accounting reasonable, but it also makes things interesting if the player doesn't play out his whole contract.

Cap Acceleration

One of the many ways the CBA helps establish parity is by keeping the accounting relatively clear of loopholes. The CBA wants to avoid any situation where teams pay a player and that money doesn't count against the cap.

So what if the team had signed Stevie to that 8-year deal and at the end of Year 2, the team felt like his play was declining so they decided to cut him in the offseason?

They paid him a huge signing bonus and it hasn't all been counted against the cap yet. This could be a potentially big loophole.

That's where salary cap acceleration comes in.

If a player leaves the team for any reason (he retires, gets cut, or suffers a career-ending injury), all the remaining prorated charges become immediately due on the salary cap.

Base salaries aren't guaranteed (except for injury or unless specified, two cases we'll get into in Part 3), so the team wouldn't have to pay him for any of the remaining years and the base salary charges would never hit the cap.

However, since the signing bonus has already been paid, it has to be applied to the cap. Since he won't be on the team in Years 3 through 8, the cap hit can't be prorated through those years. All remaining hits are immediately applied to the cap, starting in Year 3, when he is no longer on the team, but his bonus payment needs to be accounted for.

Stevie's actual pay in this scenario would be:

- Year 1: $35M ($10M base salary + $25M signing bonus)
- Year 2: $10M (base salary)
- Year 3: $0 (he's no longer on the team)

While his cap hits would look like this:

- Year 1: $15M ($10M base salary + $5M prorated signing bonus)
- Year 2: $15M ($10M base salary + $5M prorated signing bonus)
- Year 3: $15M (accelerated remaining prorated signing bonus from Years 3-5)

Now Stevie counts for $15M against the cap in Year 3, even though he isn't even on the team! This is the same cap hit he was scheduled to have, but now the team needs money to sign a replacement.

These situations can be tough to handle in the cap, but the CBA has another tool to help manage the finances: the league calendar.

The actual NFL season starts in September and the playoffs end with the Super Bowl in February. The league year (the date when the business side of things rolls over), however starts in mid-March.

Once the new league year starts in mid-March, cuts are handled like we described above (when we said Stevie was cut "when the season ends," we assumed that was after the mid-March date). But if a team wants to cut a player and has a tight cap, they can wait until after June 1st and spread that accelerated cap charge over two years.

Why June 1st?

June 1st is the magical breaking point that the CBA defined as the cut-off date for spreading out cap hits. Basically, if a team cuts a player after June 1st, they can take that full accelerated cap hit, divide it by 2, and spread it out over the next two years.

If the team had waited until after June 1st to cut Stevie, his cap hits would look like this:

- Year 1: $15M ($10M base salary + $5M prorated signing bonus)
- Year 2: $15M ($10M base salary + $5M prorated signing bonus)

- Year 3: $7.5M (accelerated remaining prorated signing bonus from Years 3-5, divided by 2)
- Year 4: $7.5M (accelerated remaining prorated signing bonus from Years 3-5, divided by 2)

This can benefit the team if they don't have a lot of cap space in Year 3, but it's only a temporary relief. The bill still comes the following year when the team is taking cap hits for a player they cut two years ago.

There is one other wrinkle to June 1 rules: a team can cut a player after the new league year starts in mid-March and give them a June 1st designation.

This means that they cut the player in March, but they pretend they did it after June 1st. The cap hit is still spread over two years, but this allows the player to look for a new team right away (before the draft in April), and allows the team to move on without sitting on the paperwork and having awkward conversations until June.

Those are all the possible implications of what could happen to the cap charges if Stevie was cut because he wasn't playing well.

But what if he was cut because someone posted a video of him doing something he shouldn't have been doing?

In cases like this, the team could attempt to make Stevie pay back some or all of the accelerated prorated signing bonus (many NFL contracts have behavior clauses like this). Similarly, if Stevie retired early, the team could also attempt to make Stevie pay that money back by arguing that he negotiated in bad faith if he intended to retire so early. In either scenario, any amount that the team recovered would be credited back to their salary cap. Everything paid has to count against the cap, but anything paid back can be credited to the cap.

Trading A Player

There's also the possibility that Stevie could be traded instead of being cut.

When a player is traded, his contract goes with him, but his outstanding cap charges remain.

In the situation above, the base salaries would travel with Stevie to his new team (when you trade for a player, you're trading for his contract), but the signing bonus would still be accelerated with his old team. His old team paid it, so they need to apply it to their cap.

Let's see how a trade would work by revisiting Stevie's original 4 year, $50M contract, which included a $10M signing bonus and $10M base salaries each year.

Here's how the actual money he is paid gets broken down:

- Year 1: $20M ($10M base salary + $10M signing bonus)
- Year 2: $10M (base salary)
- Year 3: $10M (base salary)
- Year 4: $10M (base salary)

And here is what Stevie's cap charge looks like:

- Year 1: $12.5M ($10M base salary + $2.5M prorated signing bonus)

- Year 2: $12.5M ($10M base salary + $2.5M prorated signing bonus)
- Year 3: $12.5M ($10M base salary + $2.5M prorated signing bonus)
- Year 4: $12.5M ($10M base salary + $2.5M prorated signing bonus)

Now, if he was traded after year two, he would still get paid the same amount on the same schedule, it's just that different teams would pay parts of it - like this:

- Year 1: $20M ($10M base salary + $10M signing bonus) - paid by original team
- Year 2: $10M (base salary) - paid by original team
- Year 3: $10M (base salary) - paid by new team
- Year 4: $10M (base salary) - paid by new team

But things get a little trickier when we look at cap hits.

His original team is still accountable for his outstanding prorated signing bonus, so that would accelerate once he was off the team. Assuming this happens in the offseason, after we enter the new league year, it would be a clean split like this:

Original team's cap hits:

- Year 1: $12.5M ($10M base salary + $2.5M prorated signing bonus)
- Year 2: $12.5M ($10M base salary + $2.5M prorated signing bonus)

- Year 3: $5M (accelerated remaining prorated signing bonus from Years 3 and 4)

New team's cap hits:

- Year 3: $10M (base salary)
- Year 4: $10M (base salary)

When you put them together, you see that all $50M that Stevie is paid gets accounted for somewhere. There is no hiding from the cap.

Again, this doesn't impact how or when Stevie is paid (except that the check has a different team's logo on it), but it does impact how the caps play out.

Since the signing bonus is always paid by the original team, and the cap hit accelerates with the original team, that means that the new team always gets a bit of a discount on the player as far as the cap is concerned.

So there you have it, those are the basics of how NFL contracts work.

When you break down the steps and understand why things are the way they are, it's not as complex as it seems at first.

What does get complex, are some of the advanced cap management techniques.

All dollars have to be accounted for, but teams have ways they can move that money around. Just be aware that there's no "cap magic" that gets teams out of the cap. The best you can do is move money around, but all that does is squeeze the balloon.

6

SQUEEZING THE BALLOON: CONTRACT RESTRUCTURES AND EXTENSIONS

The NFL has a hard cap, meaning that there's no way to spend more than your salary cap. You can structure contracts however you like, but you can't spend more than the limit.

If things get tough, though, there are ways to move money around.

It comes with consequences, but every year, some GMs push it.

They think they have a shot at winning it all, they think they just need a couple more players.

But they don't have any room under the salary cap.

So they restructure some deals and sign some more big-name free agents. Now everyone gets excited! Fans are booking hotels for the Super Bowl - with all these guys, we can't lose!

But wait a minute, that team didn't have any cap space. So how did they do it?

The GM must be a "cap wizard" or a "salary cap guru," or something, right?

Wrong.

All he's doing is moving money to other years so everything can fit under this year's cap.

You remember back in middle school science class when you learned "matter cannot be created or destroyed; it can only change form"?

You don't really "create" ice in your freezer, you just change the form of water.

You don't really "destroy" wood when you burn it, you just turn it into smoke and ash.

You don't really "destroy" food when you eat it, you just turn it into... well, you get the point.

There's no way to really "create" cap space either, you can just move it around.

There's a few ways a team can fit under the current cap if they want to sign more expensive players, but they always result in filling future caps.

One way is simply by structuring a new player's contract so that most of the money comes in later years.

For example, let's say Johnny Speed is signed for 3 years on a $50M deal. That's right around $17M per year, but it doesn't have to be structured with the same amount of money each year. It could be $10M in the first year and $20M in each of the next two years.

Just like we covered in Part 1, remember?

If a team really wanted to be aggressive, they could try to structure it $1M in the first year, $1M in the second year, and $48M in the third year. That may make the third year of the contract tough on the cap, but we want to win now, so who cares!?

Well, there's another problem with that.

Players like to get paid. When a contract is structured like that, the team can keep the player around for two years (at an incredibly low salary), then cut him. Salary isn't guaranteed, so they wouldn't have to pay it.

In short, the player would get screwed.

The only guaranteed money is a signing bonus. That's why players like signing bonuses.

But if a big number is put into a guaranteed signing bonus, that cap hit from the bonus is spread over the length of the deal.

That makes things tricky right?

Right, and that's on purpose. Remember that a big part of the salary cap is to establish parity. Put teams on a level playing field and it makes it easier for teams to compete. That means fans always have hope because a team can turn its fortunes around in a year. And when fans are excited, the league makes money.

The league likes making money.

So then how do these "cap wizards" and "cap gurus" make it happen?

Well, they use the same signing bonus tool that makes things so cumbersome in the first place.

Imagine Johnny Speed, is on Year 3 of a 5-year deal, making $21M per year. Let's also assume Johnny received a $25M signing bonus.

Since the cap hit for the signing bonus gets spread out and he has the same salary each year, his annual cap hit is

$26M ($21M of salary that is due each year and $5M of prorated signing bonus charge).

His actual pay by year looks like this:

- Year 1: $46M ($21M base salary + $25M signing bonus)
- Year 2: $21M ($21M base salary)
- Year 3: $21M ($21M base salary)
- Year 4: $21M ($21M base salary)
- Year 5: $21M ($21M base salary)

While his cap charges look like this:

- Year 1: $26M ($21M base salary + $5M prorated signing bonus)
- Year 2: $26M ($21M base salary + $5M prorated signing bonus)
- Year 3: $26M ($21M base salary + $5M prorated signing bonus)
- Year 4: $26M ($21M base salary + $5M prorated signing bonus)
- Year 5: $26M ($21M base salary + $5M prorated signing bonus)

This is about as basic of a contract structure as we can get. A lot of teams like to have vanilla structures like this because it makes the cap clean and usually ensures that the team isn't getting ahead of itself in spending.

Now let's say a couple years go by and the team is in a tough cap situation. The team could choose to simply not sign anyone new or they could even cut some players to ease the pressure on the cap.

But what if they want to re-sign another player on the team or bring in a pricey free agent? Well, they could go to Johnny, their high-priced superstar, and ask him to renegotiate his deal.

There's a lot of different ways he could renegotiate. Johnny could simply take less money than the $21M base salary per year - he could step up and say "I'm a multimillionaire and I care more about winning than I do about getting paid. I'm going to renegotiate my deal so that I only make $1M this year and the team has more cap money to pursue free agents and make our team better."

Well, in this case, Johnny's cap charge would be reduced to only $6M for that year ($1M salary and $5M prorated bonus charge).

Under that scenario, where he takes a drastic pay cut for one year, his actual payments would look like this:

- Year 1: $46M ($21M base salary + $25M signing bonus)
- Year 2: $21M (original $21M base salary)
- Year 3: $1M (renegotiated $1M base salary)
- Year 4: $21M (original $21M base salary)
- Year 5: $21M (original $21M base salary)

While his cap charges would look like this:

- Year 1: $26M ($21M base salary + $5M prorated signing bonus)

- Year 2: $26M ($21M base salary + $5M prorated signing bonus)
- Year 3: $6M ($1M base salary + $5M prorated signing bonus)
- Year 4: $26M ($21M base salary + $5M prorated signing bonus)
- Year 5: $26M ($21M base salary + $5M prorated signing bonus)

There's only one small problem with that plan.

You see, while this actually *could* happen, it never really does. There's one big reason for that: people like money.

Sure, there are some cases of older vets getting late in their career who renegotiate to a lower salary when their play level starts to drop and the team may be considering cutting them (or gives them an ultimatum that flat out says they need to take a lower salary or they'll be cut).

Players may agree to this for a variety of personal reasons. Some players want to stay with one team their entire career, they enjoy their teammates, or they see their last season as a chance to chase a ring one more time before retirement. Maybe they just don't want to move their families because they're invested in the community and their kids go to school there (don't forget that football players are human beings with actual lives). If their skills have waned and they want to go one more year, they can definitely negotiate a lower salary to remain with the team. Their salary goes down, but the prorated signing bonus remains.

To be clear: this can happen, but it is definitely not the norm.

Most guys want to get paid.

The career of a football player is short and once they retire, those big salaries stop rolling in.

So what can a GM do if he finds himself in the rare position of having a player who wants to get paid the contractually agreed upon salary that you signed him for?

Well, he can restructure his deal, still give the player all the money he signed up for, and also free up cap space in the current year.

He can do this by squeezing the balloon and converting some of his salary into a signing bonus.

Let's revisit Johnny Speed's situation. Johnny currently has three years left, with a $21M salary due each year. That comes out to $63M for 3 years.

Let's set aside the original $25M signing bonus (which has already been paid out and still counts as $5M against the cap each year no matter what) and just focus on this remaining $63M.

Right now, that $63M is all in the form of base salary. The original signing bonus has already been paid out and is only on the cap as a deferred, prorated charge.

If Johnny and the team agree, he can restructure that to look like a new 3-year deal that pays $1M in the first year, $1M in the second year, and $22M in the 3rd year along with a $39M signing bonus. It's still a deal that pays $63M over 3 years, but now the cap charges are spread out differently because of the bonus.

Let's start with what Johnny's actual pay will look like before we get into the cap charges:

- Year 1: $46M ($21M base salary + $25M signing bonus)
- Year 2: $21M (original base salary)
- Year 3: $40M ($1M base salary + new $39M signing bonus)
- Year 4: $1M (new base salary)
- Year 5: $22M (new base salary)

Look at that! Johnny was originally "only" going to make $21M in Year 3, but now he's going to get $40M!

That's great news for him, but how does it help the team?

The cap charges get a little trickier when it comes to restructuring a deal.

The CBA allows for restructuring a contract like this without tearing up the original contract (which would result in accelerating the original signing bonus cap charges) and signing a new one.

This is a civil agreement that allows teams to shift money around, without giving a team an unfair advantage. Since the player is staying with the team, the CBA allows this type of restructure (as long as all the money that is paid hits the cap within the scheduled parameters).

The resulting cap math can get a little more complex, though.

Since Johnny gained another signing bonus in this deal, that means there are now two signing bonuses that need to be spread over the life of the deal. The base salaries will count where they are, but those signing bonuses will be spread out from the year they are awarded to the end of the deal.

Here's what Johnny's cap charges would look like after that restructuring:

- Year 1: $26M ($21M base salary + $5M prorated signing bonus)
- Year 2: $26M ($21M base salary + $5M prorated signing bonus)
- Year 3: $19M ($5M original prorated signing bonus + $1M restructured base salary + $13M prorated new signing bonus)
- Year 4: $19M ($5M original prorated signing bonus + $1M restructured base salary + $13M prorated new signing bonus)
- Year 5: $40M ($5M original prorated signing bonus + $22M restructured base salary + $13M prorated new signing bonus)

Now, instead of a cap charge of $26M in year 3, the charge is only $19M. Same situation in year 4! It's like this brilliant GM just magically created $7M of free cap space for each year!

Is he a magician!?

No, he just moved those cap hits into Year 5, where an astronomical cap hit, larger than Year 3 and Year 4 combined, is waiting for him. Most fans, and many GMs, just push off thinking about this point until later, hoping that the cap goes up enough to cover the difference without them needing to cut anyone.

Make no mistake about it: this is a short term move with a lot of risk for a GM. He freed up some cap space for a couple years, but there's a big hit looming. If he doesn't win a Super Bowl in Year 3 or Year 4, he's gonna have a hard time improving the team with that monster cap hit looming in Year 5.

Players always love moves like this, though - they get paid sooner and look like a swell guy for restructuring "to help the team."

Now, it's true that Johnny could be cut before Year 5 and miss out on that $22M base salary, but that signing bonus of $39M is paid immediately and more than makes up the difference.

Under the restructure, he gets paid a guaranteed amount early instead of waiting for a non-guaranteed amount later. In this scenario, he makes $107M in the first 3 years instead of $88M like the original contract structure. It's still a $130M deal for 5 years, but he got paid early so even if he gets cut later, he came out ahead in the process.

This brings up another good point.

Did you ever hear the phrase "money changes people"?

Well, you might not believe this, but sometimes money changes football players, too.

Year 4 in this new deal is a pivotal year. What if, after making $107M in the first 3 years of this contract, Johnny isn't thrilled at the prospect of playing Year 4 for a piddly $1M?

He would have to be a unique type of diva to threaten to sit out or to demand a new deal so soon after signing a restructure that paid him more than the GDP of a small country. Maybe he shows up, but he's not as motivated in the offseason so he doesn't train as hard, leading to a dip in productivity. Or maybe when he gets a sprained ankle or a pulled hamstring in September, he makes a business decision on how hard he wants to try to come back and maybe he embellishes the pain to the trainer and ends up sitting out a few more weeks than he otherwise would.

After all, he's hardly getting paid at all in Year 4.

It would actually be better for him if he just got cut after Year 3 and could go sign a free agent deal with another team... and get another big signing bonus...

This is the human side to the game and it absolutely crosses GM's minds when they negotiate these deals.

Sometimes a GM still makes an aggressive move like this. Maybe there's another player on the team that he needs to re-sign. Maybe there's a free agent that he has his eye on. Maybe he just thinks it's the best way to build the team.

Whatever the case, the GM is going to have an astronomical cap hit to digest in Year 5.

Maybe.

It's possible the GM may be fired before then. When teams don't win - which often happens for reasons totally outside of the GM's control - they get fired. This is why teams are so frequently in "win now" mode: because the guys calling the shots will get fired if he doesn't win now.

In that case, the GM doesn't really care. If he made a mess of the cap by being aggressive and the team didn't win, the odds are good that the team would have lost even if he wasn't aggressive. He would have been fired anyway; the only difference is now that cap mess he made is the next guy's problem.

But what if it works? What if that restructuring

allowed the team to sign a couple key guys and they actually won?

What if we get to Year 5 and the GM hasn't been fired?

There's a big cap issue looming and Johnny Speed is gonna cost a bunch of money.

So now what?

Now it forces a decision.

The team could just cut the player. They'd no longer be on the hook for the $22M base salary. The $13M cap charge for the prorated signing bonus would remain plus the $5M cap charge from the bonus on the original contract, but that's only an $18M charge - not even half of what they'd have to pay if they kept him and incurred a $40M charge. The GM could look like a hero for cutting a guy and saving $22M on the cap. Some fans and media members actually think GMs are smart to structure contracts like this, but people who understand how the cap works know the real story (and owners don't like spending money on players that aren't playing for them).

But what if Johnny Speed is playing so great that the GM can't possibly cut him?

Well, then there's two options.

The first option is to just bite the bullet and pay the man. Keep on trucking and carry on a player with a gigantic $40M cap charge. That may be hard if you have a tight cap, though, which brings us to option two...

Sign Johnny to an extension to restructure his deal again.

At this point, the GM can think of his contract as a one-year deal for $22M (since there's nothing he can do about the $13M prorated signing bonus from the last restructure or the $5M prorated signing bonus form the original contract).

If he has an overpriced player that he can't afford to lose, he can just do another restructure - only this time, he'll add an extension to spread out the cap hit even further.

Negotiations will get tough here because Johnny (and, more importantly, his agent) knows that the team wants to keep him. He also knows that if he does nothing, the team is gonna pay $22M this year to keep him on the team.

So they can come to an agreement like a new 4 year, $88M deal. This would keep that average value of $22M in a place where Johnny feels he deserves to be paid, but structure it in a way where the team can afford it under their cap (at least in the short term, until the end comes due).

Let's say they go with a $12M bonus and a salary structure that pays $10M in the first year, $20M in the second and third years, and then has a whopping $26M salary in the final year.

This would give Johnny the same $22M payout he would have had in Year 5 (in the form of a $10M base salary and a $12M signing bonus, which is paid immediately even though it doesn't all count towards the cap), a similar salary in Years 6 and Year 7, then a big payday that he needs to work hard for in Year 8.

Now we're looking at an 8-year window that includes the 1st 4 years of the original contract, plus a 4-year extension that effectively replaces the 5th year of the original deal.

With this deal, Johnny's actual pay would look like this:

- Year 1: $46M ($21M base salary + $25M signing bonus)
- Year 2: $21M (original base salary)
- Year 3: $40M ($1M restructure base salary + $39M signing bonus from restructure)
- Year 4: $1M (restructure base salary)
- Year 5: $22M ($10M base salary from extension + $12M base salary from extension)
- Year 6: $20M (base salary from extension)
- Year 7: $20M (base salary from extension)
- Year 8: $26M (base salary from extension)

But the cap charges look like this:

- Year 1: $26M ($21M base salary + $5M prorated original signing bonus)
- Year 2: $26M ($21M base salary + $5M prorated original signing bonus)
- Year 3: $19M ($1M restructured base salary + $5M prorated original signing bonus + $13M prorated restructured signing bonus)
- Year 4: $19M ($1M restructured base salary + $5M prorated original signing bonus + $13M prorated restructured signing bonus)
- Year 5: $31M ($10M extension base salary + $5M prorated original signing bonus + $13M prorated restructured signing bonus + $3M prorated extension signing bonus)

- Year 6: $23M ($20M extension base salary + $3M prorated extension signing bonus)
- Year 7: $23M ($20M extension base salary + $3M prorated extension signing bonus)
- Year 8: $29M ($26M extension base salary + $3M prorated extension signing bonus)

Now Year 5 doesn't have that unwieldy $40M cap charge, it has a mere $31M. It looks like the GM is "creating" $9M of free money, but all he's doing is squeezing the balloon. $31M is still an enormous cap hit - the largest of Johnny's career - but it looks good because it's not as big as it was before the extension was signed.

So is it a good move?

Time will tell.

In most cases, if a player plays well or the team wins, the GM looks smart, but if the player gets hurt or plays bad, or the team loses, then the GM looks like an idiot.

This is why most mainstream media and social media hot takes on the subject are worthless. There are no right or wrong approaches, these are all just tools for GMs to use to manage their salary cap.

As fans, the best we can do is understand how the salary cap and contracts work so we can better understand and appreciate all the things that go into making a team.

Just remember that when fans on social media hail their GM as a "salary cap guru" or "salary cap wizard" when they manage to sign a guy even though they don't have cap space, there's nothing magical about it, it's just math and choosing which risks you want to take.

Let's look at a couple examples of teams that have worked on contract structure to be aggressive.

In 2013, the Denver Broncos lost the Super Bowl. In 2014, they restructured deals and brought on veteran free agents like DeMarcus Ware and Aqib Talib. With all the star power they added, they were able to win the Super Bowl in 2015.

Their GM was aggressive and pushed out cap hits and they won a Super Bowl. Their cap was in ruins after that, limiting their ability to re-sign their own players and bring in free agents. Talent levels suffered and they couldn't even make the playoffs for the next 5 years.

Many people would say it was worth it because they won a championship.

But being aggressive with the salary cap doesn't always result in a championship.

For example, after the New Orleans Saints won the Super Bowl in 2009, they lost in the Wild Card round in 2010, then they finished below .500 in 4 of the next 6 years.

At that point, they had an aging quarterback in Drew Brees and they wanted to try to win one more ring. Instead of building for the future or focusing on drafting and developing talent, they restructured deals and pushed cap space out to go all in.

They did this for years, but never made it back to the Super Bowl. When the run ended following the 2020 season, they were more than $100M over the projected 2021 salary cap.

For every team like the 2015 Broncos that loads up for a title run with aggressive cap management and wins, there are a dozen like the 2020 Saints.

They all end with cap issues, but occasionally they get a ring for their trouble.

It's up to each GM to decide how aggressive they want to be.

As fans, all we can do is understand it so that we can enjoy and appreciate the journey a little more.

7

HOW SALARY IS PAID OUT

U p until this point, we've looked at base salary as one large number that is paid out each year.

That's the easiest way to think about it to understand the cap, but in practice things get slightly more granular.

Signing bonuses are paid as one big lump sum, but annual salary is not. If a player makes $2M in base salary for a season, he doesn't get one big $2M check when the season starts.

Instead, that $2M gets spread out over the 17 weeks of the season. Each week, a player making $2M in base salary would get a check for 117,647.06 (which is $2M divided by 17).

Likewise, if a player is making $17M per year in base salary, he would get a check for $1M each week.

That salary is not guaranteed, which means if a player is cut or traded in the middle of the season, the remaining salary would not count against the team's cap.

Teams have to account for every dollar they pay out in the cap, but they don't have to account for dollars they don't pay. Obvious, right?

For example, if Timmy Quarterback signed a 4-year deal that paid $17M of base salary each year and had an $8M signing bonus, his planned cap hits would look like this:

- Year 1: $19M ($17M of base salary + $2M prorated signing bonus)
- Year 2: $19M ($17M of base salary + $2M prorated signing bonus)
- Year 3: $19M ($17M of base salary + $2M prorated signing bonus)
- Year 4: $19M ($17M of base salary + $2M prorated signing bonus)

But if Timmy's play dropped off and he was cut after the 8th week of Year 3, his cap hits would look like this:

- Year 1: $19M ($17M of base salary + $2M prorated signing bonus)
- Year 2: $19M ($17M of base salary + $2M prorated signing bonus)
- Year 3: $12M ($8M of base salary + $2M prorated signing bonus + $2M prorated signing bonus accelerated from Year 4)
- Year 4: $0

Under this scenario, Timmy's actual pay by year would be:

- Year 1: $25M ($17M of base salary + $8M signing bonus)
- Year 2: $17M (full year of base salary at $1M per week)
- Year 3: $5M (5 weeks of base salary at $1M per week)
- Year 4: $0

Now, if Timmy was traded after 8 weeks of Year 3, everything above would be true, but his new team would owe him $9M in Year 3 and $17M in Year 4 (his remaining base salaries) if he was on the team the whole time. The signing cap proration and acceleration would still be owned by Timmy's original team.

PART III

RULES, THEORIES, AND CASE STUDIES

8

OTHER BONUSES

I n Part 2, we used signing bonuses as the main vehicle for understanding how contracts work and are applied to the cap. The reason signing bonuses are unique is because they are the only bonus that has a prorated cap hit. This makes understanding them a bit more challenging and gives teams a lot more flexibility in cap management.

There are a lot of other types of bonuses, but they are all straightforward in that they are paid and capped in the same year they are earned (with one possible exception that we'll explain towards the end).

All bonuses are optional items to include in a contract.

Workout Bonuses

These are simple. If a player shows up to and participates in a minimum number of the team-scheduled workouts, the player gets paid.

The bonus is paid in a lump sum and hits the cap in the year it is paid.

These bonuses can be used as a way to make sure players stay in shape or may just be another way to give a player future earning options.

Roster Bonuses

Roster bonuses are like mini-signing bonuses that players can earn simply by being on the team at a specified date. Often, the first day of the new league year is the specified date, while the first game of the season is another common date.

A player could receive an annual roster bonus in their contract terms instead of a signing bonus. This would give the team some flexibility - if they cut a player, any future roster bonuses wouldn't need to be paid and wouldn't accelerate into the current salary cap.

However, if the player is traded, their contract is traded with them - including bonuses - so the new team would be responsible for paying the future roster bonuses to the player if they're on the team on the specified day.

These bonuses are less desirable for players than signing bonuses, but give them an incentive to perform well.

Per-game Roster Bonuses

Per-game roster bonuses are similar to regular roster bonuses, but are paid out in smaller increments. A player could get an $800k roster bonus for a year, meaning that they would get $50k for each of the games they are on the roster for.

Sometimes, teams will pay these only if a player is on the 46-man active gameday roster. This would be an incentive for the player to play well enough to earn some playing time.

In other instances, teams will pay these if a player is on the 53-man roster for the week, even if they're inactive. In this case, the bonus protects the team from having to pay a player if he is injured (since base salaries are guaranteed for injury - which we'll talk more about later).

Likely To Be Earned (LTBE) And Not Likely To Be Earned (NLTBE) Incentives

Likely To Be Earned and Not Likely To Be Earned Incentives are the fun bonuses that can be added to contracts.

These can be for anything, really.

A player can have a bonus for making the Pro Bowl, scoring 10 touchdowns, or having at least 50 yards in each game.

They're like the prop bets of NFL contracts.

They can be for any dollar amount, too. If a team wants to give a running back a $10M bonus if he gets one carry during the year, they can (I don't know why they would, but nothing is stopping them).

The only difference between these various performance bonuses is how the "likely to be earned" ones are handled on the cap differently than the "not likely to be earned" ones.

So if Timmy Quarterback gets a $1M bonus for throwing 30 TDs, how do we know if it's likely to be earned or not likely to be earned?

The NFL doesn't look at the gambling odds on prop bets, they take a much easier approach: if the player accomplished the feat the previous year, it's considered "likely to be earned" and if he didn't accomplish the feat the previous year, it's considered "not likely to be earned."

So if Timmy Quarterback threw for 29 or fewer TDs last year, this would be considered a not likely to be earned incentive (NLTBE). However, if he threw for 30 or more TDs last year, this would be considered a likely to be earned incentive (LTBE).

Very neat.

But why does this matter?

Because of the salary cap.

If a bonus is considered a LTBE bonus, then the amount of the bonus counts against the current year's cap. If the player doesn't earn it, that amount is credited back to the cap to be rolled over the following season.

If a bonus is NLTBE, then it wouldn't count against the current year's cap. If the player doesn't earn the incentive, nothing happens. However, if the bonus was actually earned, it would be applied to the following year's cap.

Let's look at how this could play out with Timmy Quarterback's $1M bonus for throwing 30 TDs.

Let's say Timmy Quarterback threw for 22 TDs in Year 2 of his deal and he has a $1M bonus for throwing 30 TDs in Year 3.

This is considered a NLTBE incentive since he didn't throw for 30 TDs in Year 2. So if Timmy doesn't throw 30

TDs in Year 3, nothing hits the cap. However, if Timmy does manage to throw 30 TDs, he gets a check for $1M and the team gets a negative $1M cap adjustment for Year 4.

Note that the player's cap number doesn't change because the bonus was earned in Year 3 and the Year 3 cap was already calculated. Instead, the team cap is adjusted for the following year (remember in Part 1 when we talked about rolling over unused cap space? This is like a deduction from that rollover).

If Timmy has that $1M bonus target for throwing 30 TDs in his contract every year, his Year 4 cap number will actually go up by $1M (because that Year 4 bonus target is now considered LTBE).

So when Timmy hit that NLTBE incentive, he reduced the team's cap for next year by $1M *and* increased his own cap number by $1M for next year. In this way, any time a player hits an NLTBE incentive that is on their contract every year, it effectively feels like a double hit to the cap if it is ever met.

Performance incentives like this are great for motivating players, but that kind of volatility in the cap can be tough to manage.

Salary Escalators

If the cap volatility of performance incentives is something a GM is concerned about, they can go with salary escalators instead.

These are like the LTBE and NLTBE performance bonuses, but instead of being paid out as a bonus in the year they are earned, they trigger an increase in the future base salary of a player.

Let's say Timmy Quarterback has a performance escalator in Year 2 of his contract that says if he throws for 4,000 yards and the team makes the playoffs, his base salary increases from $8M to $10M.

If Timmy throws for 4,100 yards and the team makes the playoffs, he doesn't get an immediate guaranteed bonus like the incentives described above. Instead, his base salary for the following year goes up from $8M to $10M. However, if anything happens that prevents him from earning his base salary (he retires, is cut, etc.) he does not get paid that money (and it doesn't count on the team's cap).

And yes, Virginia, there is such a thing as a salary de-escalator. Timmy Quarterback could also have a clause in his contract that says if he throws for less than 2,000 yards, his base salary could actually be reduced the following year.

Playoff bonuses

Players on teams that make the playoffs get additional bonuses as a simple reflection of their team's success (motivation generates competition, which makes the league more entertaining and therefore more profitable).

Following the 2020 season, every player on a wild card team earned a $30k bonus ($33k if their team had won their division), players on teams that made it to the Divisional round each got $33k, and teams that played in the conference championships got $59k per player. Super Bowl losers got $75k, while the winners each got $150k.

These bonuses come directly from the league as a part of a separate funding pool, so they do not count against a team's salary cap.

This is another part of establishing parity and breeding competition.

If a team in the playoffs lost a player to injury, and they were at or near their cap limit, and couldn't afford to sign a replacement, competition would suffer.

But when a team signs a player during the playoffs, they are effectively free (unless they get a signing bonus). Base salaries are only paid out during the regular season and playoff pay comes from a central pool that doesn't impact a team's cap.

So if a veteran is sitting around doing nothing and a playoff team calls them because they need an injury replacement, the player gets to join the team and chase a ring while the team doesn't have to worry about the salary cap.

9

OTHER RULES

As if we haven't been through enough rules, there's more. That's not just because lawyers wanted to make things more difficult, though - these all serve a purpose. Understanding these finer points of the CBA and how they impact the salary cap helps us better understand the subtle balance between all the factors involved, which helps us better understand why teams do the things they do.

Rookie Rules

Rookies have some stricter rules to play by when it comes to contracts.

Many years ago, when rookies came into the league, the first thing they had to do was negotiate their initial contract. But it's hard to place a value on a player who has never played a down in the NFL.

Players would hold out for bigger deals, stunting their

growth and hurting their teams. There was even a time when teams would try to sign players before the draft even started so that they would have a deal in place if the player fell to them.

All that stuff is in the past.

The CBA now defines almost all aspects of the rookie contract deals based on what slot a player is chosen in.

All contracts for drafted rookies are 4-year deals and the base salaries and signing bonuses are standard, with higher picks making more money. This makes it easier for teams to plan and manage their cap and also makes sure the player gets in to start developing and set himself up for the best career possible instead of holding out for a better deal.

Players selected in the 1st round get a 4-year contract like all the other rookies, but they also have a built-in team option for a 5th year (which features a more generous salary).

Additionally, players drafted after the 1st round have Proven Performance Escalators built into their contracts. These state that if a player participates in a certain percentage of their team's snaps in two of their first three seasons, or they make the Pro Bowl, their 4th year salary will automatically increase.

Since this increases their base salary, this also impacts a team's salary cap and is another reason why having extra space in the cap is a good idea instead of spending the max amount each year.

Top 51 Rule

During the regular season, NFL rosters are limited to 53 players (not including the practice squad).

In the off-season, when teams have rookies and tryout players coming to camp, rosters expand to 90 players, allowing teams to evaluate more players and generate competition in training camp.

Teams always have to stay under the cap though, every minute of the year, so how do they do it when they have so many more players on the roster?

Through an offseason exception known as The Top 51 Rule.

The bottom of the roster fluctuates a lot in the off-season and there's no real advantage for a team to be gained by working out more players (and accountants don't want to do a lot of unnecessary paperwork), so the CBA dictates that only the 51 largest cap hits on the roster "count" in the off-season. It's a simple way to make the offseason easier for everyone.

Once the rosters are finalized and teams all have to cut down to 53 players, all of the cap hits (including practice squad players) need to fit under the salary cap.

Veteran Salary Benefit

When players negotiate for the CBA, they have their best interests in mind, which leads to some interesting clauses.

Think about the slotted rookie wage scale. In the past, rookies could make way more money, which would lessen the amount of cap space available for veterans. So the veterans voted to limit rookie salaries (to a fair amount, just not an exorbitant one). College players don't vote on this, so they couldn't say no - it was pretty brilliant on the part of the veterans.

The Veteran Salary Benefit is another clause that the players put in the CBA to protect themselves and is a very rare exception where dollars paid out don't count against the cap.

Yes, I said that every dollar paid out has to count against the cap, but I also said that lawyers negotiated the CBA, so there were bound to be exceptions. This is the biggest one.

This rule states that a veteran with four or more seasons of experience can sign a 1-year minimum deal (with a small limit on any type of bonuses) and count for less against the cap than they are actually paid.

Why do veterans need this?

All players have a minimum salary that they have to be paid. The more seasons a player plays, the higher the minimum salary gets (i.e., the minimum salary for a guy with 4 years of experience is much lower than the minimum salary for a player with 8 years of experience).

So if an older player who isn't a superstar looking for a huge contract just wants to keep playing, this salary exemption makes it easier for him to compete for a roster spot with much younger players (who have much smaller minimum salaries).

When managing the cap, teams are often torn between keeping an older player who has proven to be solid or replacing him with a younger, unknown player who has a lower cap hit.

This rule also helps specialists like long-snappers stick

around. If an old vet playing 10 years would count against the cap for the large 10-year veteran minimum, teams may not want to spend that much money for a guy who only plays a handful of snaps each game. Teams often keep bringing in rookies and younger players in for specialist roles like this.

The Veteran Salary Benefit makes it easier for teams to retain players like this and makes it easier for veterans to stay in the league.

Injury Settlements

One of the differences between football and other sports is that NFL contracts aren't automatically guaranteed, except for injury.

This means if a player is injured during the season, he is still entitled to receive his base salary for the time he is injured that season (though he may miss out on things like performance bonuses).

However, if a team doesn't want to keep an injured player on the roster and keep paying him while he's hurt, they can negotiate an injury settlement.

This is basically the team and the player agreeing to terms on about how long the injury would keep the player out for, paying them for that timeframe, and cutting them immediately.

For example, let's say Scrubby Williams is on a one-year deal making a base salary of $850k with a $100k signing bonus.

Let's say Scrubby breaks his leg in Week 4 and his prognosis is that he will miss two to three months.

The team wasn't planning on re-signing him next year and he's going to miss most of the season, so they'd prefer to just cut him. This can't be done without an injury settlement.

The team and the player (and his agent) need to agree on a fair number of weeks that his injury would probably keep him out. Let's say they agree that the broken leg would keep him out of football for 10 weeks.

Scrubby's base salary of $850k comes out to $50k per week, so the team would need to write him a check for $500k (the $50K that he would be paid for each week times the 10 weeks that they agree the injury would probably keep him out for) in order to cut him.

This money will count against the cap the same way it would if he was on the team for that time.

In all, Scrubby's cap hit for the year would be $800k ($100k signing bonus + $200k for the 4 weeks he played + $500k injury settlement).

Once he is cut, Scrubby is free to sign with another team as soon as he can find a suitor.

Suspension Pay

Sometimes players do things they aren't supposed to do. Occasionally, this can result in a suspension.

When a player gets suspended in the NFL, he's suspended without pay. When a player doesn't get paid, it doesn't count towards the cap.

So if Timmy Quarterback posts something deemed socially unacceptable on social media and gets suspended for two weeks, his pay - both base salary and prorated signing bonus - don't count against the cap. Timmy won't be receiving those two game checks and he will have to pay back a portion of his signing bonus.

In this scenario, if Timmy Quarterback is making $17M in base salary and has a prorated salary cap charge of $3M for the season (based off a hypothetical $15M signing bonus on a 5 year contract), he would miss out on $2M worth of game checks ($17M base salary divided by the 17 weeks of the season times the 2 weeks he will miss) and will have to pay back almost $353k of his signing bonus (the $3M prorated signing bonus for the year divided by the 17 weeks of the season times the 2 weeks he will miss).

It may be harder for the team to win the next couple of games while Timmy is suspended, but on the plus side, they'll save over $2.3M on the salary cap for that season.

10

GAMES AGENTS PLAY

C ontracts are about more than just the pay.
There's a game behind the game behind the game when it comes to agents and negotiating contract structure and numbers.

As fans, the more we understand about the contract game, the more we can understand our favorite team and the decisions they make, and the more we can enjoy football.

When a new contract is announced, it's usually just the number of years and the maximum value. But in most deals, the maximum value is never earned. When the first breaking headlines come out for a new contract, it's a good idea to wait until the full structure and details are released before passing judgement.

For example, what if a headline came out that Scrubby Williams, some backup you barely heard of, got a 4-year contract for $107M - would you be shocked?

It seems like way too much to pay for a backup. That's almost $27M per year!

But what if it isn't?

What if the contract had no signing bonus and structured the base salaries like this?

- Year 1: $1M
- Year 2: $1M
- Year 3: $5M
- Year 4: $100M

This contract could just as easily be a 2-year deal for $2M or even a 3-year deal for $7M dollars.

But there is no way any team is going to be paying any player anywhere near $100M in a single season any time soon.

That may be a bit of an exaggeration, so let's look at a more plausible contract.

Let's say Scrubby Williams has been a backup for the first 4 years of his career and he's getting ready to sign a new deal.

What if his deal had no signing bonus and looked like this?

- Year 1: $1M base salary + $1M incentive for starting 16 games
- Year 2: $1M base salary + $5M incentive for making the Pro Bowl
- Year 3: $1M base salary + $5M incentive for making 1st or 2nd Team All Pro
- Year 4: $10M base salary

This is a heavily incentive-laden deal that we can look at from both sides.

From Scrubby's side, a $1M base salary is so-so salary for an NFL backup. However, if he becomes a starter, a Pro Bowl player, or even an All Pro, he can make a lot more money. If he plays well enough that they keep him around for the 4th year, he can really cash in!

If Scrubby truly believes in himself and realistically thinks he can do those things, this might look like a good deal. If he doesn't think he can hit those incentives, it's still at least a so-so deal for a backup.

From the team's side, the fact that there's no signing bonus makes it a very neat contract to manage, regardless of how Scrubby plays - they can cut him at any time without having to worry about accelerated cap hits. The $1M base salary in the first 3 years is very reasonable for a backup that knows the team's system. The bonuses are big, but they play into the team's hand.

In Year 1, the odds of a guy who has been a backup for 4 years suddenly becoming a starter for all 16 games seems unlikely.

If Scrubby makes that unlikely jump, the team pays him a total of $2M, which is cheap for a 16-game starter. If he makes the Pro Bowl or All Pro in Year 2 or Year 3, he gets paid $6M. That's a lot more than he was scheduled to make, but it's basically a bargain for a Pro Bowl level veteran.

By Year 4, the team will know if Scrubby is worth $10M or not. It's unlikely that he would be after being a backup for so long, but if he made it to an All-Pro level by then, it's actually a reasonable salary for an upper-echelon player. If not, the team can cut him with no cap impact, since Scrubby didn't get a signing bonus.

This is a very team-friendly contract that lets the player bet on himself.

In almost all likelihood, though, this is, at best, a 3-year deal for $3M for a backup player.

So why would they even bother with a contract like this?

The game behind the game.

Media and public perception may not help teams win football games, but they can help teams, players, and agents.

This gets reported as a 4-year contract with a maximum value of $24M.

Now, Scrubby Williams is in the news as a former backup who is now getting $6M per year (even if that isn't totally true). Instead of being perceived as a bench-warming nobody, Scrubby is seen as a guy making some solid money.

Casual fans hear his name more and maybe start to know who he is - "Holy cow, Scrubby Williams just got $24M - he must be better than I thought!". At the very least, he'll be a more recognizable name when his playing days are done and he's signing autographs at the Ramada Inn. It sounds silly, but this is an absolute reality of life for guys who don't achieve superstar status.

Scrubby's agent looks good, too. Sometimes when a contract comes out, they also announce the agent, especially if it's a contract getting a lot of attention (like a career backup getting a contract for solid starter money). When Scrubby's agent is looking for new clients, he now gets to say things like "Hey, I'm the guy that got Scrubby Williams $6M per year - imagine what I can do for someone as talented as you!" This also sounds silly, but it is a big part of how agents get new clients.

Then there's the team that gave Scrubby this new contract. Some people might snicker at a team giving a backup such a large contract (though people who understand how these things really work will get it), but in reality, this is a selling point for future free agents. When a player has a choice on which team he wants to play for, will he go to a team with a reputation for responsibly managing their cap... or the team that gave a backup like Scrubby Williams a 4-year deal worth up to $24M?

Putting these kinds of deals out can benefit everyone. They don't happen all the time, but when a contract is announced, it's always a good idea to wait until the full details are published before passing judgement on it.

Heavily incentive-laden contracts can be used in other situations, too - like a consolation prize or ego soother.

Let's say an aging vet with deteriorating skills just finished his second contract and didn't get picked up through the main free agency period. He wants to play, but doesn't want to look like an old-timer taking a big pay cut. At the same time, some team wants to show that they value and believe in him (to motivate him to play better), so they offer him a deal with a lot of incentives.

Don't forget that players are humans, full of emotions and often get a chip on their shoulders for motivation.

11

THE CHEAP QB SIREN SONG

I n managing an NFL salary cap, a team's biggest cap hit is almost always its starting QB.

QB is the most important position and is almost always the highest-paid (and rightfully so, as they impact the game more than any other position).

It's great to have a good QB, but a good QB can eat up 10-15% of a team's cap. For a sport with more than 50 players on the roster (an average of less than 2% of the cap available for each player), that can present some challenges in fielding a competitive team.

A theory has emerged in the media and NFL fandom that a young QB on a rookie deal (which are limited as a part of the CBA), is a franchise's best chance to field a championship team.

That's a great theory, but let's see how reality has played out. Here's the quarterbacks that have squared off in the last half dozen Super Bowls:

- 2020: Tom Brady (on a big free agent deal) and Patrick Mahomes (on a contract that made him the highest paid player of all time)
- 2019: Jimmy Garoppolo (on a big extension after being traded) and Patrick Mahomes (on last year of rookie deal)
- 2018: Tom Brady (making big bucks) and Jared Goff (on rookie deal)
- 2017: Tom Brady (making big bucks) and Nick Foles (on a free agent deal)
- 2016: Tom Brady (making big bucks) and Matt Ryan (on a huge contract)
- 2015: Peyton Manning (on a free agent deal) and Cam Newton (on a huge contract)

So in the last 6 years, a quarterback on a rookie deal has only made the Super Bowl twice. That's two out of twelve.

That's way lower than the league average for how many teams typically have a starting quarterback on a rookie deal.

Prior to that, guys like Drew Brees, Aaron Rodgers, and Eli Manning were all beyond their rookie contracts and making big bucks when they won Super Bowls.

So what does that tell us?

It tells us that this over-hyped idea of having a quarterback on a rookie deal isn't nearly as important as having a good quarterback and a good team. Look at the rosters for those Super Bowl teams and you'll find them jam packed with Pro Bowl talent at plenty of positions besides quarterback.

And the only way you get a great roster like that is by having a well-managed cap.

It's why this topic is so intriguing and so important to the game.

Football is too complex and difficult to just say "Let's get a cheap quarterback and spend big on free agents" and expect to win. The league of chock-full of teams that have tried and failed.

It's very hard to win without a good quarterback, but the fact that having a cheap quarterback makes it easier to win is a theory that has not played out.

12

CASE STUDIES IN CONTRACT STRUCTURE

All this theory is great, but Scrubby Williams and Timmy Quarterback aren't actually NFL players (sorry if I misled you). So let's look at a couple real-life examples of unique contracts and explore how they came to be.

Jared Goff

Remember when we talked about guaranteed money in Part 2? That had a big impact on the Jared Goff trade that went down after the 2020 season.

The Los Angeles Rams led the NFL in scoring offense in 2018, averaging 33 points per game. Jared Goff appeared to have full command of Head Coach Sean McVay's cutting edge offense.

All the way up until the Super Bowl that is.

After putting up pinball numbers all year, the New England Patriots brought in a defensive game plan that rendered the Rams offense entirely impotent, holding them to 3 points - the lowest ever recorded in a Super Bowl.

The Rams regressed the following season, but Goff still had a productive year, racking up over 4,600 yards passing in McVay's offense.

With the 5th year option looming on Goff's contract, the team had a decision to make. They could let him play out the final year (in which case a great season would mean they would have to pay an enormous contract or risk losing him) or they could try to sign him to an extension while there was still a year left on his deal, allowing them some leverage.

They opted to sign Goff to a 4-year extension worth $134M.

But this wasn't one of those crazy incentive-laden deals like the Scrubby Williams scenario we outlined earlier.

This included a $25M signing bonus. Now, for a quarterback, this isn't huge or abnormal.

What was abnormal was the fact that Goff had guaranteed salaries totaling $65M in the first 3 years. That's in addition to the $25M signing bonus!

Goff looked mediocre his first year after signing this extension. He got hurt late in the season and the Rams actually won a playoff game with their backup quarterback. When Goff returned to action the following week, they lost and were eliminated from the playoffs.

That was when the Rams realized that Goff wasn't their guy. They needed him off the team.

The problem was that if they wanted to cut him, they

would accelerate nearly $90M of cap hits from all his salary guarantees. That was more than half of the projected cap for the following season.

If they wanted to trade him, they would need to find a team willing to take on all his salary guarantees. His signing bonus was already paid by the Rams and the cap hit wouldn't be passed on to any team that traded for him, but his remaining $43M in salary guarantees would.

But if a team was actually going to play him as their starter (which the Rams were not going to do), that money would be spread out over the contract as base salaries and not accelerated into one year as a cap hit all at once (like it would be if the Rams cut him).

That was what made the situation so unique and fascinating.

In the end, the Rams and Lions agreed to swap starting quarterbacks. The Lions took Jared Goff and his obnoxious contract, while the Rams got Matthew Stafford in return. However, the Lions also took two 1st round picks and a 3rd round pick from the Rams to even things out.

The quarterbacks had roughly similar levels of talent and salaries, but because Goff's contract was so atrocious, they had to send a huge bounty of picks over for the Lions to agree to take the contract on.

In the end, the Rams had to trade a 26-year-old quarterback who had recently been to the Super Bowl for a 33-year-old quarterback who had never led his team to a playoff victory or even a division crown - and they had to send a couple of 1st round picks and a 3rd round pick to do it!

And the kicker is that Goff's signing bonus accelerated

to hit the Rams cap, costing them another $22M in dead cap. They had to send two 1st round picks and a 3rd round pick to get his contract off their books and it *still* cost them a $22M hit to their salary cap!

This is how damaging it can be to a team to mismanage the cap by signing players to bad contracts.

Patrick Mahomes

Unlike Jared Goff, who made it to a Super Bowl in his third season and laid an absolute goose egg, Patrick Mahomes went to the Super Bowl in his third season, won the game, and was named the MVP.

So his case was a little different.

When he entered his 4th year, the Chiefs knew they had to lock him up.

The problem was that Patrick Mahomes had one of the most impressive starts to a career as any quarterback had ever had and his abilities put him in the conversation for best player in the league at a very early age.

In other words: he wasn't gonna come cheap.

He also didn't want to get stuck in small 3- or 4-year deals that would leave him needing to negotiate new contracts over and over.

In the end, the Mahomes and the Chiefs agreed to the largest contract in the history of football: a 10 year $450M extension with an additional $25M in incentives. To make it easier on the cap, the extension was signed when he was still under contract for up to 2 more years, making the window on the deal 12 years.

As we've seen in most of our examples, teams use

signing bonuses as a tool to manage cap hits. But signing bonuses can only spread cap hits over a maximum of 5 years, so they would need to be creative with Mahomes's contract, which now had a length of 12 years.

Despite the enormous size of the deal, the signing bonus was only $10M (which is a lot of money, but not for a guy of Mahomes's value).

That meant a meager $2M was spread over each of the first 5 years of the deal, leaving another $440M to figure out how to structure.

As a player in a violent sport with a limited earning window, Mahomes wanted some assurances.

The contract ended up paying Mahomes relatively small base salaries early on. In the first 7 years, his base salaries only range from $825k to $2.5M. However, these are offset by roster bonuses ranging from around $22M to nearly $39M.

That means that if Mahomes is injured in any of those years, he will still get paid nearly all of his money for that year. It's a rare kind of security that's only afforded to a young superstar like Mahomes.

In the 8th year of the deal, Mahomes will turn 32 and the team will have a bit of a decision point. In that year, Mahomes is due a $10M salary and a roster bonus of more than $49M. Throw in a little workout bonus and he would be paid just shy of $60M.

That number is ludicrous based on the salary standards when it was signed, but the salary cap will probably go up by then, which the team is betting on. The question is: how much?

No one knows, which is why such long contracts are difficult to negotiate.

However, after Year 8, his total compensation numbers decrease to between $44M and $52M per year.

These are big numbers, but may not seem so big in the future. The nice thing for the Chiefs is that they can cut him at any time and have no cap impact since their guarantees are all paid out far earlier in the deal.

This lack of guarantees late - especially the absence of a signing bonus beyond Year 5 - also makes it way easier to renegotiate the deal.

This is probably what the team plans on (and probably the player, too, if he's being honest with himself).

This contract takes advantage of having 2 years remaining on Mahomes's current deal, which spreads out the early cap hits. Then, everything beyond that is a pay-as-you-go model without any guarantees, which makes it easy to cut him (which seems unthinkable given how he has played early in his career) or renegotiate the deal.

In the long-term, the contract just serves as a framework for the future that is very easy to change later. It's a really smart way to lock up a superstar quarterback long term with a very flexible deal and logical decision points. In many ways, it's the exact opposite of the Jared Goff contract which took a quarterback with a lower talent ceiling and gave him a short-term contract structured with very little flexibility.

13

WRAP UP

Football is a great sport. It's beyond great - it's the most complex and entertaining spectator sport of all time.

The on-field strategy, drama, and excitement, coupled with the constantly evolving game strategy, is more than enough to keep us glued to the TV every week for four months of every year of our lives.

But to really understand and appreciate it, you have to understand how the salary cap works and how it drives team development.

I truly hope you enjoyed this book and that it helped you understand how the cap works and how it drives the game of football and your favorite team's decisions.

I want to thank you for taking the time to read this and truly hope it helped you appreciate this game that we love.

I also want to give a special thanks to Ken Ingalls (@KenIngalls on Twitter) for clarifying some of the deeper points so I could make this the best book possible (please note: Ken didn't check all my work, so if something is wrong, it's probably from me!).

If you'd like to see more of my football coverage, feel free to follow me on Twitter at @PackersForTheWn or check out my website at PackersForTheWin.com.

THANK YOU

Thank you for reading!

I truly hoped you enjoyed delving deeper into NFL Free Agency strategy and history.

If you enjoyed this book, would you please consider leaving a five-star review? This link will take you to the page:

PackersForTheWin.com/ReviewSalaryCap

Reviews are the lifeblood of any book. Your review can help others find this book, in addition supporting me.

Thank you so much,

-Bruce

ABOUT THE AUTHOR

Bruce Irons is a fan of football who has watched, played, coached, studied, and thoroughly enjoyed the sport for decades.

You can read more of his analysis at:
    PackersForTheWin.com

You can also follow him on Twitter:
    @BruceIronsNFL

BOOKS BY BRUCE IRONS

A Fan's Guide To Understanding The NFL Draft: Strategies, Tactics, And Case Studies For Building A Professional Football Team

A Fan's Guide To NFL Free Agency Hits And Misses: Case Studies And Lessons From Landmark Signings Throughout History

A Fan's Guide To Understanding The NFL Salary Cap: How The NFL Salary Cap Works And Why It Matters

Made in the USA
Monee, IL
28 May 2022